FIX YOUR CREDIT NOW

For Better Credit and Higher Scores

Claudette M. Pendleton

INTRODUCTION	3
GETTING STARTED	8
APPLYING FOR CREDIT AND PAYING YOUR BILLS	13
CREDIT CARD BALANCES	14
CREDIT COUNSELING & DEBT CONSOLIDATION	17
DEALING WITH CREDITOR HARASSMENT	18
RE-ESTABLISHING CREDIT	20
MAINTAINING YOUR CREDIT PROFILE & SCORES	23
SOMETHING ELSE TO CONSIDER	26
HOW TO STAY CREDIT ALERT	27
ONE LAST WORD	28

INTRODUCTION

Fix Your Credit Now for Better Credit and Higher Scores is a great resource to help consumers reflect and think about how to better manage their finances. It consists of several easy steps to follow and some very good tips to apply in one's daily life. It is a practical guide to help consumers rebuild their credit profile and increase their credit scores!

NOW is the time to take charge of your credit and take back what belongs to YOU! It is time for you to have better credit and higher credit scores.

So…Why put off tomorrow what you can begin to do TODAY!

FIGHT AND WIN THE GOOD BATTLE OF FAITH!

NEVER, EVER GIVE UP!

KEEP PRESSING UNTIL YOU REACH YOUR GOALS!

Good to Excellent Credit creates better self-esteem and greater confidence!

IMPORTANT DISCLAIMER

Fix Your Credit Now for Better Credit and Higher Scores is NOT INTENDED TO SERVE AS A SUBSTITUTE FOR LEGAL ADVICE. It is imperative that you consult with a licensed legal attorney if you require legal advice.

Fix Your Credit Now for Better Credit and Higher Scores is only a guide to aid consumers in credit restoration and is not to be considered a guarantee that a consumer's credit scores will increase nor is it a guarantee that a consumer's credit profile will be restored. Credit profile restoration and credit score increase is the sole responsibility of the consumer.

Hi, I'm Claudette Pendleton, the author of *Fix Your Credit Now for Better Credit and Higher Scores*. I believe that *Fix Your Credit Now for Better Credit and Higher Scores* will help many to establish a better credit profile for themselves as well as a chance to become more aware to manage their finances well. I know how it feels to be overpowered with debt and not have enough money to pay bills and then, of course, just to end up with serious credit issues. As a result, and even prior to becoming a Certified Credit Counselor, I used what I had learned from my own mistakes, over the years, to restore my own credit profile.

I had finally decided to become committed to working on my own credit profile. At first, I would pay others to work on my credit profile just to end up very disappointed and frustrated. Several people just walked away with my money and did absolutely nothing to help my credit profile, and two of them at least started to work on it, but then began to quickly slack off and each time I ended up with very little results or none at all. So, yes, after all of that, I finally decided to take control of my own credit destiny, realizing that no one will ever care about my credit profile quite like I will!

Life's trials can throw any one of us off course at any given time, but I am so thankful that we can be restored again and again whenever we find ourselves off course when we choose to be committed to better our lives. We don't ever just have to stay in the same old negative circumstance! We have the power and ability to change our own lives! The change may certainly require a process, but the point is... change happens if we want it bad enough. Even when it doesn't seem like it, know that you're making progress and continue to press in for the full manifestation of the change you are hoping for!

At any rate, after much prayer and thought, I was impressed to establish the *Fix Your Credit Now for Better Credit and Higher Scores* e-book. It will serve as a guide to help people clear up the negative items on their credit reports so that they can begin to enjoy the benefits that come with having a better credit profile, higher credit scores, and commitment to making wise credit and monetary management decisions for themselves going forward such as seeking to obtain credit at low interest rates instead of at ridiculous high interest rates and not applying for and using too much credit.

So many times, we do absolutely nothing about restoring our credit profile simply because we tend to believe that we must be able to pay off everything at once to accomplish a better credit profile. But this is not true. It is crucial that you start somewhere. If all that you can do is pay a little at a time concentrating on one debt at a time, then do just that and then move on to the next one until you have accomplished your credit goals, but the solution is to start somewhere and to be consistent.

Many people also believe that after having to file for bankruptcy, there is absolutely no hope for their credit profile ever again. But this is also a misconception. Even after experiencing bankruptcy being placed on your credit reports, you can still begin to rebuild good credit so that your scores can begin to increase again. You must look at it positively and consider it to be a fresh start because that's just what it is - A Fresh Start for you.

Nonetheless, I do realize that just the thought of starting any project can be overwhelming, but the fact remains that we are the only ones who are responsible for our own success in life. No one else is responsible for our own individual success and no one else will care about your credit profile or financial status quite like you! If we don't take charge and move forward on our own behalf, things will more than likely remain the same! So, even though it feels like it's just too much to deal with to restore your credit profile, the fact remains that you must take charge of your own life because we are the only ones who can make what we desire happen.

God Almighty has created us with the ability and power to accomplish whatever we truly believe in and set our hearts and minds to do, but with this awesome ability and power, it is important to remain humble, grateful, and thankful. Gratefulness, thankfulness, and humility are always essential regardless of where we are in our lives! Maintaining a humble, thankful, and grateful attitude of the heart carries the power within it to bring us back on top of bad circumstances and, sometimes, even quicker than we expected.

One more thing, always remember as the good book states, "It is better to give than to receive." This is because it helps us to steer away from becoming too self-serving. So, once you've mastered your credit goals and have paid off your debts, you are empowered at that point to begin to help someone else: your family members, friends, church, missions, ministries, or charities to help people who are less fortunate.

However, it may be a good idea to start this giving practice even before all your debts are paid off. Even a little bit helps and helping others can create joy in the heart and opens new doors for the giver. After you've re-established your credit and financial situation, you'll be able to make a difference in someone else's life as well!

I believe that if you follow *Fix Your Credit Now for Better Credit and Higher Scores*, you will be pleased with the end results. Remember; Determination is essential to accomplishing your credit restoration goals. My best wishes to you as you embark on your credit restoration journey! So, let's get started!

"FIX YOUR CREDIT NOW"
For Better Credit and Higher Scores

GETTING STARTED

The very first thing to do is order your credit reports. On your credit reports, you will see your personal information, account information, public record data, and inquiries.

1. Order your credit reports from the three (3) major credit-reporting agencies. You can order them via the regular mail system or via the internet. Because the following addresses are subject to change, it is best to confirm the addresses and phone number prior to ordering your reports.

   Trans Union
   P.O. Box 2000
   Chester, PA 19022
   800-916-8800

   Equifax
   P.O. Box 740256
   Atlanta, GA 30374-0241
   866-349-5191

   Experian
   P.O. Box 4500
   Allen, TX 75013
   888-397-3742

When requesting your credit reports or disputing an item on your credit report, you will need to provide:

- Your full name
- You complete mailing address
- Your date of birth
- Your social security card and number
- Your driver's license
- The name of the creditor and account number if you're disputing an item
- The reason for your dispute or disagreement
- Your signature
- You may also need to send a copy of a utility bill

If you're requesting your credit reports via the internet, you may need to answer some questions regarding your credit history to prove your identity.

According to the Fair and Accurate Credit Transactions Act, consumers have a right to receive one free copy of their credit reports annually.

Otherwise, you will need to pay for a copy or you will need to have been, recently, denied credit, insurance, or employment to get a free copy of your credit report. It may be a good idea to send your request via certified mail if you're choosing to order your reports via the mail system. Keep copies of all paperwork that you send out and receive.

You can log onto http://www.annualcreditreport.com and obtain a free copy of all three of your credit reports, <u>once a year</u>, from the three major credit-reporting agencies (Trans Union, Equifax, and Experian).

You can also order two of your credit reports online at http://www.myfico.com. At this website, you can receive both your TransUnion and Equifax credit reports *and* your FICO credit scores when you receive your credit reports. Consumers must pay a nominal fee to get their scores and reports from myFICO.

To get your Experian credit report and the score that Experian calculates for consumers, you will have to get them directly from Experian, but know that the score you receive from Experian may be considerably different from the score that lenders get from Experian to determine credit worthiness. This is because most lenders generally use the FICO scoring system in their decision making whether to grant credit to consumers. They do not use the credit scoring system used by the three credit reporting agencies. The credit reporting agencies' scores are provided to consumers to give an idea of what the score could be.

The credit scores that creditors/lenders use to determine your eligibility for credit, when you apply for credit, are called Fair Isaac scores. FICO is an acronym for the name Fair Isaac Corporation. The name came from the last names of two men who created this popular credit scoring system that most lenders use and as mentioned prior, your FICO credit scores in addition to your credit reports from TransUnion and Equifax can be purchased at www.myfico.com.

Once you have all three of your credit reports and as you follow *Fix Your Credit Now for Better Credit and Higher Scores*, you will be able to track your progress and not only observe how your credit profile and scores have improved.

Important Note: If you choose to purchase the two credit reports and scores from www.myfico.com, you may want to come back to this website periodically and repurchase your credit reports and scores as you pay off your debts and/or dispute items to make sure that your creditors are updating your new information on your credit reports and to see how much your scores have increased.

However, if you prefer not to repurchase your scores and reports periodically from www.myfico.com, you can, of course, choose instead to continue corresponding via regular mail, online, or by telephone with the three credit reporting agencies to make sure that your credit reports are being updated, but keep in mind you will not receive your FICO scores from the Credit Reporting Agencies.

Nevertheless, if you can see that your credit reports are being updated, your scores should also increase as a result.

2. Organization is key to accomplishing your credit and financial management goals. So, it's a good idea to maintain file folders for your credit reports and for all other relevant information.

3. Once you receive your reports, review the reports, and take note of the accounts that are delinquent and need to be paid off. Then, make a list of all delinquent accounts by name, the account number and write the information in a journal or notebook that's designated specifically to your credit goals. Also, if there are any items that are incorrect on your reports, you can either dispute the item online at www.annualcreditreport.com or at www.myfico.com if ordered from these sites, but keep in mind that Experian reports cannot be

purchased from myFICO.com. Therefore, you may also choose to write to each credit-reporting agency to dispute the items that are incorrect, or dispute by telephone. Make sure that you include all pertinent information in the letter when writing.

NOTE: *It will depend on which method you use to order your reports.* Once the items are removed, corrected, or paid off, your credit scores should also increase accordingly.

Whether you receive your credit reports via www.annualcreditreport.com or via www.myfico.com, you should receive a code to log back into your account for a designated period of time so that you can dispute any items that you believe are erroneous.

To dispute items over the phone, you must have a current report with a confirmation number on it to give to the representative. Your confirmation number will be on your credit report. There is also a specific number to call to dispute items over the phone and it should be listed on your credit report as well.

APPLYING FOR CREDIT AND PAYING YOUR BILLS

It is imperative that you do not apply for any credit or pay your bills late while you are in the process of disputing items and/or working toward increasing your credit scores and restoring your credit! Applying for credit and paying your bills late can lower credit scores! Remember: it is your final responsibility to accomplish your credit restoration goals.

So, remember to pay all bills on time if you can. Paying your bills on time every month maintains your credit scores and as a result your credit scores will gradually continue to increase as well.

CREDIT CARD BALANCES

If you can, pay your credit card balances in full every month. By doing this, your credit scores will very likely increase quicker from this practice. If you cannot pay them in full every month, work toward paying down your balances to at least half of the credit limit.

Not allowing your credit card balances to exceed more than half the amount of your credit limit allowance is also another way that your credit scores may increase. (Example: if your credit limit is $1500.00, it would be a good practice not to allow your balances to exceed $750.00. However, many experts suggest not using more than 30% of your available balance; the lower your credit card balances are, the better).

4. After writing down the creditors' phone numbers and the account numbers from your credit reports for each delinquent account, call each creditor and ask for a settlement. That is, *if you can pay in full a lower amount offered to you by the creditor.* It won't harm you to ask. Sometimes people have not because they ask not! Find out if your creditors will agree to allow you to pay a lower amount to settle the account in full. Whenever you can pay an account off in full, it is always a good idea to find out **first** if they will agree to a settlement offer; a lower amount for you to pay. Many companies may accommodate you in this way and especially if the account has been delinquent for quite some time. Don't forget to notate all information to keep track of everything and to stay organized. Keep in mind that organization is vital.

5. It may be a good idea to begin to pay off accounts that have the smallest balances and then work toward the larger balances. If you can pay off smaller accounts in full, then this may be the best way to go about it. This may also keep you motivated as each small account is paid off. As you pay off smaller accounts, your credit scores should begin to rise and should be noticeable. If all that you can do is pay a little at a time concentrating on one debt at a time, then do that but, certainly, do not just do nothing. Start working on your credit and keep going. You will see progress if you remain focused on your goal. You must stay positive and have faith to accomplish your goal!

6. After you have paid off the smaller account balances, it is now time to begin working on the larger accounts. You may have to make arrangements to pay these larger accounts, but please don't forget to ask for a settlement first *if you can pay <u>in full</u> the amount that they may offer.* Some creditors may be more agreeable to a settlement when they know the debt will be paid off in full.

Some people prefer to tackle the larger mountain of debt first and then the smaller ones. It's your choice. The point is, you are taking charge of your credit and rebuilding your credit and every time you make a payment (small or large), you are chopping down and destroying that old debt. And as you chop down that old debt, your credit profile will begin to look better and, yes, your scores will increase as well!

Keep in mind that rebuilding credit is a process and that it also depends on an individual's situation and the available funds that each person must work with. However, in the end, it will prove to have been a wonderful process and something to celebrate about all because you decided to take charge of your credit situation!

7. As you pay off your delinquent accounts, continue to monitor your credit reports. Make sure that your creditors are updating the information that you are disputing as well as the debts that you have paid in full. You want all of this to report accurately on your reports. As you receive updated reports and new correspondence from the three credit reporting agencies, be sure that all necessary changes have been made.

CREDIT COUNSELING & DEBT CONSOLIDATION

If you don't think you really have the discipline needed to pay off your debts yourself or maybe you just don't feel like being bothered with any of it and you wish that it would all be much simpler, then you may want to consider a credit counseling service or debt consolidation.

Credit Counseling Services provide counseling to consumers regarding their credit and debt problems. Their services may also include gathering from you all your debt information and negotiating with your creditors to obtain a settlement or agreement to lower or remove all interest so that you will have a lower amount to pay the creditor. Once this is accomplished, you will pay the credit counseling service a specified monthly lump sum amount and the organization will then make payments to each of your creditors for you.

Debt Consolidation is provided by a lender. So, the lender grants you, the consumer, a loan amount to combine all your debts to pay off all of your creditors. The debt consolidation company hence becomes your one new creditor.

The payment may be a considerably lower monthly payment after consolidating all your debt. You can search for reputable credit counseling services or debt consolidation companies over the internet and acquire more detailed information about each of these types of services to explore your choices more thoroughly, but of course, the choice is finally up to you!

DEALING WITH CREDITOR HARASSMENT

The Federal Fair Debt Collection Practices Act shields and protects debtors from creditor harassment. It is illegal for creditors to oppress, intimidate, harass, or abuse debtors regarding collecting a debt.

A few examples of illegal harassment from a creditor are as follows:

- Threatening a debtor by using violence in any way or form with an intention to implement physical harm

- Threatening a debtor with the intent to harm his or her personal property, reputation, or family members

- Harassing a debtor by using obscene language

- Repeatedly phoning a debtor with the intent to harass, irritate, and annoy the debtor as well as to abuse the use of the debtor's telephone number at home or at his/her work environment

If you are in a situation where you simply don't have the funds to pay a creditor, it is best to at least contact the creditor to explain your situation and let the creditor know when you can pay on your debt.

However, if the creditor begins to intimidate and harass you in their attempt to try and collect the debt from you, as a debtor, you may want to consult your attorney about having a "cease & desist" letter sent to the creditor. You can also send a cease-and-desist letter yourself; however, it's always a good idea to consult with your attorney first about any legal matter. A "cease & desist" letter will instruct the creditor not to make any further contact with you. After receiving the letter, the creditor by law is prohibited from contacting the debtor except for in certain limited situations. If the creditor ignores the letter and chooses to violate the rights of the debtor according to the Federal Fair Debt Collection Practices Act, the creditor could be reprimanded and punished substantially.

Once the calls of harassment have ceased and you can think more clearly, use this time to brainstorm to come up with additional ideas and ways that will help you to continue to work toward paying off your creditors to rebuild your credit.

RE-ESTABLISHING CREDIT

If you have filed for bankruptcy in the past or are in a situation whereas you have unfavorable adverse credit items on your credit reports, you can still begin to rebuild your credit profile. It may be a good idea for you to apply for a <u>secured</u> credit card and begin to rebuild some good credit this way to increase your scores. A specific amount of funds placed in a savings account at the bank secures the credit card that's distributed to you by the bank. You can apply for a <u>secured</u> credit card while you are in the process of paying off your old debts.

By doing this, future creditors may look at your new and good credit and view you as a potential consumer that can be trusted to grant credit to because of your newly established credit profile that shows a positive payment history.

Of course, there is no absolute guarantee that *every* creditor will be convinced to grant you credit, however, re-building your credit is a positive thing to do to be open for new opportunities. Your new credit profile and the fact that you will have paid off or is in the process of paying off your former debts may be a strong incentive for creditors to consider granting and trusting you with credit again.

A secured credit card is a credit card that requires a security deposit. Many of the banks require a deposit as low as $200 to be placed into a bank savings account. However, it can be higher according to the credit limit you would like.

The bank will grant you credit equal to and according to the deposit that you make into the savings account. This is to protect them from any loss just in case the consumer defaults in paying back the balance on the secured credit card. This is also a way to make sure that you don't have to worry about paying the debt off if you were to ever experience future financial trouble. A savings account secures the debt. So, you could easily just instruct the bank to pay the debt with the secured savings that was deposited in the bank.

To help rebuild your credit profile, the bank will report the monthly balance and payment activity on the credit card to the three-major credit-reporting agencies and consequently your credit scores should increase.

If you have a bank account, check with your bank to find out if they offer secured credit cards. You can also check with local banks in your area to learn more about the banks that grant <u>secured</u> credit cards to help consumers re-build their credit. However, some banks grant <u>unsecured</u> credit cards as well to give consumers a new start toward rebuilding a new credit profile.

However, *as you search, be sure to compare interest rates as well as annual fees, and any hidden fees. You want to choose the best card with the lowest interest rate and the lowest annual fee or even better - no annual fees at all. Keep in mind, the higher the interest rate, the more money you will pay for the cost of credit to you. You will also want to compare the differences in the cost of late payment fees and over-the-limit fees. But, of course, there will be no late payments or using the credit card so much that you're running over the limit, right? And finally, also, make sure that the bank reports to all three-major credit-reporting agencies because this is how your credit profile will be re-established as well as how your credit scores will begin to increase!*

The credit activity must be reported every month. Remember: It is so vital to be disciplined in managing your finances and spending this time around as you re-establish your credit.

MAINTAINING YOUR CREDIT PROFILE & SCORES

Many factors are involved in establishing credit scores and every individual's situation is different. The main aspects in determining your credit scores will include:

- your overall credit payment history
- the amounts you owe on accounts
- the number of accounts with balances
- how long you've had the balances
- the length of credit history
- any newly established credit and
- the various types of credit used

Having credit cards and/or other types of credit can result in having too easy access to open credit and this can be very tempting for some. There are several things a consumer can do to maintain good credit:

- Pay bills on time each month as agreed; late payments, collections, judgments, etc. have a negative effect on a consumer's credit scores.

- Be careful not to apply for credit unnecessarily; It can be very, very tempting, but keep in mind always that credit scores are often lowered when you apply for excessive credit.

- Avoid credit inquiries; again, avoid applying for credit unnecessarily. <u>Too many credit inquiries can lower credit scores</u>.

- However, when shopping for a mortgage loan or car loan, there are exceptions to the rule.

Having multiple inquiries for the same type loan due to shopping and comparing <u>mortgage interest rates or car loan rates</u> within a 30-45-day period, generally, will not hurt your credit score. However, some experts suggest that the period is within a 14-day period.

- Having multiple inquiries for the same type of loan within this period are looked upon as a single inquiry because it is generally understood that you will have just one mortgage loan or just one car loan after shopping for the best rate. However, this same principle does not apply to applying for credit cards or other types of credit.

- Keep balances low on credit card balances and on other "revolving credit" and if possible, choose to pay them off in full each month or keep the balance low. Some experts suggest that it is best not to use more than 30% of your available credit. Most importantly, avoid high credit balances.

- Avoid having too many accounts with high balances. Even though you may pay everything on time, you may be viewed as a credit risk by having too many credit accounts with balances remaining.

- Make sure payments are made on time over a period of time. The *longer* the account has been opened and paid on time with low balances maintained, credit scores should increase accordingly.

- Re-establish a positive payment history with creditors who have negative items on your credit report.

- Work toward paying off debts and then maintaining a low debt profile.

- Do not close unused cards thinking it will raise your credit score. If balances remain on closed accounts, it may lower your credit scores. Maintaining a good credit history counts. So, it may be best not to close accounts even though you've paid the account balance in full.

- Establish new and positive credit but remember not to apply for too much credit which can result in having too many open accounts. Having too many credit inquiries and/or too many open accounts can lower credit scores.

- Consumers should check their credit reports periodically. Scores will not be affected when consumers request their own credit reports. If errors are detected, they should be corrected by contacting the credit reporting agencies as well as the lenders as soon as possible.

SOMETHING ELSE TO CONSIDER

1. After 7 years have passed, negative adverse credit should fall off your credit reports. (After 10 years if it's a bankruptcy). However, sometimes the adverse credit is not removed automatically, and it is still negatively affecting your credit and scores. Contact the Credit Reporting Agency and request that all negative credit that is over 7 years old be removed from your credit report. Once the negative information is removed, your credit scores should also increase as a result.

2. If you have had a few late pays reported on your credit report, you may be able to negotiate with the creditor and ask if they will agree to remove the negative late pay information after you have paid on time for approximately 6-12 consecutive months. If they agree to your request, after all terms have been met by both of you, your credit scores should increase.

3. Many consumers do not know that they can request to have missed payments or unpaid car and/or mortgage payments placed at the end of the loan or request to have their payments lowered for a period of time; if for some reason a hardship is experienced. These requests are, more often than not, granted to a consumer due to hardship issues that the consumer may be experiencing. Remember: It's all in the asking!

HOW TO STAY CREDIT ALERT

Knowing what's going on with your credit is very important and it can be done by signing up with a credit monitoring service. There are several to choose from, so it would be a good idea to research several credit monitoring services before choosing one.

A Credit Monitoring Service will monitor your credit reports for any activity or changes to your credit reports and will notify you when any activity and/or changes have occurred on your credit reports. This is a great tool to have because this type of program helps consumers to remain alert and to become aware of what's going on with their credit reports at all times. Some credit card companies also offer this service to their customers.

ONE LAST WORD

If you begin to experience problems along the way after working on your credit profile, do not become discouraged, throw up your hands, and decide to give up. Just start again where you left off, continue to implement what you have already learned, and begin to continue rebuilding your credit profile. I know it can be frustrating when setbacks occur but know that you can overcome any obstacle that comes your way when you believe and remain persistent!

NEVER GIVE UP!

The race is NOT given to the Swift,
Nor the battle to the Strong,
Nor bread to the wise,
Nor riches to men of understanding,
Nor favor to men of skill
But time and chance happen to all!

Therefore,
Use your time wisely and
Take your chances!

Best Wishes!

www.ingramcontent.com/pod-product-compliance
Lightning Source LLC
Chambersburg PA
CBHW031600210526
45464CB00003B/1366